Perpetual Patterns

Neil N. Chopra

SHADOW
SCRIPT

http://www.neilnchopra.com (@shadownnc)
http://www.perpatterns.com (@perpatterns)

Published by Shadow Script
P.O. Box 53, Diablo, CA 94528
shadowscript@neilnchopra.com

Cover design by Trevor Ragan

Printed in the United States of America
ISBN-13: 978-0-9850860-0-8
ISBN-10: 0985086009

To my family,
Vinod, Kanchan, and Monica

Those things we know
And try to say
They sing and float
Inside our brain
But if we show
The pattern's trail
We'll break the flow
Of muted wail

Contents

Introduction

I'm the kind of person who likes to stay quiet unless there's something of use to say. What I enjoy about this behavior is it allows me to spend time paying close attention to anything and everything around me. Over the past several years, these observations have been running through my mind unchecked, without any sort of release. So I started writing them down. In the beginning, it was simple bullet points and rudimentary poetry about particular subjects that came to mind, but even that alone was a wonderful experience. There was something very liberating about writing it all down so I didn't have to worry about remembering their details. As time went on, these thoughts coalesced around the idea of describing patterns, good and bad, that I see in my own and other people's behavior, and it started to look like a book.

Before I go on, I want to say that I highly encourage anyone else who has *any new idea* whatsoever to follow suit. Stop thinking and write it down. Thoughts are fickle creatures. When you ask for them to come back as you remember them, they often hide in the recesses of your mind. You will find that once you write an idea down, you are forced to really think about it in concrete terms. Keep in mind that you shouldn't waste time worrying about getting it down **perfect**. It doesn't matter where or how you do it, just *that* you do it. You can always change it, as long as you have *some* record to come back to. While working on this book, wherever inspiration hit, I would write something down.

Now, back to the actual patterns, which I think are best explained by something that happened during the course of writing about them. I was on my way home one day finding myself really angry about a small thing someone did that I felt served only to garner more attention toward themselves. So angry that I couldn't get it out of my head and felt I needed to sit in my car and write an extra paragraph on **recognition** that explained the audacity of those who crave attention even when there is nothing of substance behind it. It didn't help, I still couldn't get the event out of my head.

Later that night, I read my bullet points about **resentment**. To my surprise, I was so consumed with pointless rage that I had completely forgotten the *words I had written myself* not but a few days earlier when I started this project. Every bullet point I skimmed through exactly described the pattern I had fallen victim to once more. It calmed me down, got the scene out of my head, and made me rethink whether that extra spiteful paragraph about recognition was actually a positive addition. It was at that point I realized this was the format I wanted this book to be in. An organized, simple reflection on patterns I've observed around me, that I myself have unconsciously slipped into. Every word should have a purpose and be carefully chosen so there is no **noise** or wasting of space and time. Anyone with a mind to could quickly read about a single pattern within a couple minutes, and immediately see whether it resonated with their particular situation.

In addition, I've found that exposing the truth in something often requires simply asking the right question. Your preconceived notion about an idea or topic can be turned on its head with a good question that causes you to think about it in a different light. Your honest answer to a question might end up being radically different than what you expected. Closing each chapter is a series of questions that is meant to help gauge whether or not a pattern has actually manifested.

Finally, each chapter begins with a poem. This may seem a bit odd and out of place, but I've always felt that when you force yourself to creatively express an idea through some constrained medium, like short lines that rhyme, you gain a deeper understanding of it. These poems have helped me anchor the essence of each chapter, and are meant to paint a picture that isn't really possible with straightforward explanation. Maybe there will be particular verses that stick with you more so than the content of other sections. All of these aspects of a chapter are meant to complement each other, hopefully they accomplish that.

There will be no anecdotal stories from my life. Each excursion is meant to logically and visually give you something to think about, and remain applicable no matter what time or situation you come back to it in. You will notice references to other chapters (all in bold) throughout the book, they are meant to emphasize the overlap of these patterns. A note on sequence: I deliberately chose the order in which the patterns are presented, focusing on the darker poetry and deeper issues near the end, but feel free to jump around where your interest takes you. I hope you eventually do explore all the content of each chapter. The final one, on

reciprocity, will attempt to tie everything together and bring a conclusion to the book.

My hope is, through reading this, you look at the world from a slightly different perspective, or at least start thinking about things you didn't consider before. Maybe it will provide a spark for you to reflect on your own thoughts. I am a firm believer that everyone alive has a unique take on the world, and we are all better off having the opportunity to learn from it. I strongly encourage you to find some way to creatively express your ideas, whether it is through poetry, music, painting, film, game design, comedy, or any other of the endless varieties of artistic communication. Whatever you feel works for you is exactly the path you should take. This book is what works for me.

❧ Discovery ❧

The water tempest awakes
The waves crashing my ship
The wind swirls in my face
The wheel firmly in grip
The destination may have been set
But I ache to explore
I want to play on the jets
Not quickly anchor at shore
This weather may capsize me tonight
Splintered wood will be left
But I'll have seen all the sights
Without a hint of regret
You described how it is to dive
In an unknown, remote cave
But I can only feel alive
If I go and do the same
This map I clutch I have ignored
Though it surely would be of help
With a shrug I throw it overboard
I think I want to draw one myself

The journey is far more important than the beginning or the end.

A journey should be embarked upon out of a joy for what you are unexpectedly going to discover. It should be voluntary, not forced. It should be riddled with excitement for what you will see, hear, touch and feel that you haven't before. It should allow your imagination to run wild. Its worth should *not* be measured by its outcome. When you play in a sandbox, you are experimenting with what you are capable of and makes you tick. However it concludes does not have a bearing on the journey itself. When the end is your only focus, you are setting yourself up for disappointment. Revel in the journey, savor in the surprise.

When shortcuts are taken, or help is required, the experience is tainted. You have a much more profound understanding of what you've discovered when you are able to do it on your own at your own pace. It certainly will take longer, but every obstacle and challenge will be vividly remembered and appreciated. What you learn can be applied to countless situations. Having something handed to you does not come without cost, you've relinquished your right to a feeling of accomplishment.

Having your own experience allows you to come to your own conclusions. You needn't rely on descriptions provided by others, unless they are taken with a grain of salt and are meant to further calibrate your own opinion. It is impossible for someone else to put themselves in your shoes in such a way that their experience can be a substitute for your own. Your mind is absolutely unique. Nobody who has ever lived or will ever live can duplicate the *exact* reaction you have when you experience something. Skipping that experience is not only detrimental to yourself, but cheats the world of the viewpoint you can bring to the table, the unique interpretation you've created.

It is natural to want to reap the rewards of an effort sooner rather than later. It is also natural to forget what you learned in the process when met with failure, and instead look for **blame**. If you change your mindset to one of adventure, where the focus is on what you will discover, your momentum to attack new challenges will never run out. There will never be a sense of **boredom**. Any success will be welcomed, then set aside as you start anew. Any failure will just be an invitation to try again.

Situational Questions

- Are you ruining the surprise for someone else? Would it not be a greater reward to be a silent observer and share the joy they will feel when they discover it on their own? What do you gain, and what do they lose, from your desire to be **recognized** in their journey?

- Are you dissuading someone from having their own experience based on your recollection of what you went through? Would you rather have your opinion **validated** without opposition? What if they see it differently than you?

❧ Formality ❧

The velvet rope unhooks
When we slowly bow our head
We seldom hope to look
Upon the face that we all dread
We walk along the carpet
A straight and narrow path
To talk or venture off it
Will kill our slender chance
We knock three times and wait
As we were told to do before
We hope we are not late
As we stand silent at the door
We hear deliberate footsteps
From the other side
We hold our breath, my goodness!
Is it finally our time?
The door swings wide and all we see
An empty space within
We lower our eyes towards our feet
An infant with a grin!

Formality can be taken to such lengths that it becomes childish in itself.

The simplest example of formality is one person being in charge of a group of people. In this situation, it is less important *who* is in charge and more important *that someone* is in charge. The formality is allowing more efficient delineation of responsibility. When that turns into the leader clinging onto power with a sense of **superiority**, believing only *they* can be in charge, regardless of their utility to the group, a change should be made. An honest leader is not afraid to follow someone else when it is more beneficial to others.

Process is good, but only when it is helping achieve a goal that is hampered by a lack of process. Each time complexity is introduced, it should be grounded and focused on the end goal it helps facilitate. The introduction of process for the sake of it should never be a goal itself. When formality is based on logic and has a clear goal in mind, it will be more widely accepted.

Furthermore, when the actions of entrepreneuring adults are stymied because of a strict hierarchy and rigid adherence to process, too much formality is in place. They should be trusted to follow the *intent* of a decision. They should have the flexibility to step outside the process if it allows them to more efficiently attain the primary goal at hand. This behavior, which in real-time allows experiments that produce better results, should be encouraged and rewarded, not dissuaded.

Dissent should not be punished, **obedience** in opinion should not be forced. Honest adults should be allowed to publicly disagree with a decision, while still carrying it out. It is insulting to assume an individual cannot make a distinction between their own reservations and the necessity to follow the order. Environments that focus on consistency of results, instead of homogenizing opinions, foster new ideas that move goals forward.

If there is no logical backing for an existing formality or tradition, it should be phased out. If there is a genuine push to make ideas better, everything should be on the table, even tried and tested formalities. Conversely, if it is a tradition that is simply making people happy and doesn't have any negative consequence, it's reasonable to leave it alone. Focus should be directed towards those that are having an adverse effect on an important goal. Often, symbolic formalities get too much attention and distract from what can lead towards an actual positive outcome.

Situational Questions

- Are you trying to thwart the removal of a rule because its existence is beneficial to you? Is the rule based on any logic? Does it actually provide a benefit to others, or are you reaching for justification because of the **comfortable** situation it maintains for you?

- Do you enjoy joking around, being on both the giving and receiving end? Or does decorum cause you to condemn and avoid humor? Are you so self-conscious that you aren't able to roll with the punches?

❧ Normalcy ❧

Houses lined across a row
Patterns of pleasing colors
A mirror would be enough to show
No need to see each other
But one stood out amongst the rest
Its owner was given a notice
The group had thought that it was best
For no one to get all the focus
When that scheme failed, they laughed out loud
In unison when they walked by
Like moths to lights they did surround
Couldn't match husband and wife
He cut his grass without looking up
And went on with his business
Then told the mass, "You should give love
To those who seem so different."
He offered an axe to every one
Even the women and children
And said, "Relax and have some fun
Tear down your house and rebuild it!"
They took his advice and swung so free
Creating an image they'd chosen
All shapes and sizes across the street
Lived in by minds wide open

Embrace uniqueness.

Normal is subjective. What you consider abnormal may be perfectly normal for someone else. What you find normal may be perplexing for someone else. The tendency to want to be perceived as normal doesn't take into account the variety of perceptions you will face. Understanding this subjectivity can help break the trend of going the typical route.

Being in an environment where everyone is the same can be suffocating. If your goal is to continually learn, there is no better way than to be immersed in diversity. It is impossible to experience everything first hand (though that route should always be preferred), but learning to see the world through someone else's eyes, someone who is different from you, will show you things you didn't think were possible.

Regardless of your surrounding environment, living a template that has been laid out by someone else can also be suffocating. Your choices are limited. Your movements are restrained. Your freedom to explore what might really interest you is suppressed. You shouldn't shy away from being different, you should embrace the opportunity to blaze your own trail. On the other hand, you also shouldn't do something different just for the sake of being different. It needs to *mean* something to you, even if there will be no **recognition** for it. This balance of finding your unique path without worrying about how others interpret it is important.

Continuing down this notion of recognition, it is natural to want to be accepted, to want to fit in. On the surface, there is reward in being welcomed into a group of like minded individuals, but it should not be an ultimate goal. A much more profound instance of acceptance occurs when you are so true to yourself, so unequivocally sure of who you are, that others gravitate towards you. Not because you have done something for them, not because you are similar to them, but because you've exposed them to something they haven't seen before. No two people are exactly alike, and their unique characteristics and dimensions should not be tolerated, they should be celebrated.

It is natural to be scared of something different. It is easy to look at something from afar and choose to dismiss it because it is of a different language, a different accent, a different color, a different location, an entirely different culture. It is also not unreasonable to think that it may be difficult to fully understand the complexities of that culture, to a point where even if you wanted to be immersed in it and be accepted, it would be impossible. What is easy to understand, however, what is easy to appreciate, is what the culture means to those who practice it. For those who have an aversion to cultures foreign to them, take the first step of respecting its meaning. For those who anxiously want firsthand experience of something new, take a step back and begin by respecting its meaning.

Situational Questions

- Do you go to great lengths to *look* different? If nobody was able to see you, would you still go through the trouble? What in particular about your appearance means something to you, regardless of how you are perceived?

- Do you geek out on anything? Do you love something so much that you get more and more excited as you delve into every detail of it? Do you avoid expressing this feeling openly for fear of not being looked at as normal, or because the subject itself isn't considered normal?

- Are you immediately critical of anything new? Is your attachment to what you are used to preventing you from seeing the worth of what has come along? Are you afraid your own way of thinking will become obsolete?

❧ Boredom ❦

She talks so much, more and more
About these things so useless
Her chalk is rough while on the board
How much longer can she do this
I stare outside and see the swings
They call for me inviting
I want to climb between the rings
The horse begs me to ride him
This sheet in front confuses so
It looks like gibberish
It seems to only prove I know
A tiny little bit
She stands behind, her pencil worn
And draws a swing through the equation
She flips one to other, born
Into a new location
The paper asks to take my pick
I can hardly seem to stay down
In a sudden flash it all just clicks
Now this is my new playground

If you open your eyes, everything is interesting.

If you are lucky enough, you have found a passion of which you revel in the details. You enjoy voluntarily learning new things concerning that passion. When you come across something that doesn't fit its scope, though, you may shrug it off as a waste of time. Even if what you are experiencing doesn't fascinate you on its own, know that some lesson from it can be derived that connects back to what *does* interest you. Absorbing something in the context of applying it to what you already know will give it a new dimension. You may even see what you already know in a different light, or through someone else's viewpoint. There is always something to learn.

Every experience is meaningful. Each one further enlightens what you know about yourself. Good experiences show you what you want to strive for. Bad experiences show you what you don't want to become. Exciting experiences show you what gets your heart pumping. Boring experiences show you what requires more patience. In the quest to understand who you truly are, ignoring what is in front of you, no matter how boring it may be, is a terrible mistake. If you approach each situation as an opportunity to master what is most important to you, no encounter will be taken for granted.

Boredom can lead to **desertion** because you are giving up on the creator of the experience. If you attempt to see it through to the end, you may come across something you didn't expect. You may even be able to give constructive feedback that can improve the experience in the future. If you enter a situation with the understanding that there is always *someone* behind it, you can change the focus to giving that individual a full and honest chance to prove themselves. Imagine how much more useful both of your experiences will be, the creator receiving positive reinforcement, the audience paying close attention to provide such reinforcement.

A natural inclination is to be attracted to the famous, the powerful, the rich. They all overtly have something that is interesting to many, and that in itself interests you. It is tangible, it is right in your face, it cannot be ignored. However, narrowly focusing on these novelties desensitizes you to the rest of the interesting things in this world. Indeed, the stories behind notoriety are often less interesting than the struggles people go through every day. It is important to dig for the meaningful truth buried behind the glamour.

To be fair, these are all difficult things to do. It is much easier, and more natural, to simply abandon an experience that doesn't interest you, or is not suiting your taste. But understand that such an act is taking away from your own **discovery** of the world, and of yourself.

Situational Questions

- When someone explains to you what their passion is, are you engaged? Can you think of questions to delve deeper into what means something to them? Can you derive a lesson from what they're saying and apply it to your own life? Or are you nodding along hoping it will end soon?

- Do you choose to not approach difficult topics because you feel they may be out of your league? Have you had someone else explain them at a high level to you? Have you tried starting out by understanding their building blocks?

- Have you had trouble figuring out what really interests you, what you want to pursue? Do you focus on the ends more than the means of getting there? When trying your hand at something new, do you ask yourself whether you would still do it even if you weren't compensated for it?

❧ Blindness ☙

I sprint down the road
The end in my sights
Momentum explodes
I veer to the right
The fork to my left
Went by in a flash
A sign up ahead
But time I don't have
I fly through the ribbon
Exhausted and proud
Is the podium hidden?
There must be a crowd
Deserted in front
And on either side
Burnt under the sun
With hands at my eyes
You mentioned the track
Wasn't as easy as this
I'll trudge my way back
And see what I missed

Be aware.

It is easy to disregard the context of information and warp its meaning into something it is not. There is a tendency to try to meld your interpretation of the truth so that it facilitates reaching your own end. Your narrative reflects observations that reinforce your choices and justify your mistakes. Know that such a reality is very fragile. You will have to avoid anyone that doesn't **validate** your viewpoint. You will have to ignore anyone that challenges it. It will eventually come crumbling down if you are blind to the full realities of the situation. When you are aware, and are able to articulate your awareness, more people will be receptive to your conclusions. If your honest, underlying motivation is to seek the truth and make choices not shrouded in **obscurity**, you should go out of your way to achieve awareness.

Details are the beating heart of anything of value. These details are guaranteed to be observed by *someone*, and your lack of attention troubles them. Your lack of recognizing their understanding of the details and giving weight to their opinion troubles them. It is true that it may simply not be possible to personally address everything. Being a master of details does not require you to have a thorough understanding of *every* aspect of *every* subject. A sufficient first step is to acknowledge that there are important pieces of information you may not fully grasp, and that giving credence to those who do have the understanding is worthwhile. Eliminating the **noise** generated by your own ambition (and the ambitions of others) is key to discovering the details that matter.

This is not to say you should succumb to your surroundings and not have a vision for what you want to get done. There is a distinct difference between being obedient and being aware. If you can pursue your goal without it becoming your narrow focus, if you can understand your environment without losing sight of that goal, these skills will complement each other and meld into a unifying talent. You should unconsciously absorb your surroundings while still giving priority to your task at hand.

All actions have consequences. When you sit on a throne of **comfortability**, where you are immune to the repercussions of your actions, it is easy to be blind to the cascading effect they have on others. Make sure that connection is not severed. Make sure you can not only see, but *feel* the consequences. Awareness is best achieved by going through the pains yourself.

Situational Questions

- If someone explains something to you, are you able to articulate it back to them to their satisfaction? Do you try to end the conversation quickly, or persist until you have a full understanding of what they are trying to say? Are your questions geared towards extracting what you want to hear, or exploring the actual truth?

- When you walk into an unfamiliar place do you take notice of the details around you? Are you more interested in locating things you recognize or getting accustomed with the things you don't?

❧ Awe ❧

I see her sit down at the table
Her bag drops with muffled thump
She reaches for her favorite fable
The bookmark shows she's almost done
Her hair shimmers as it flows
Her fingers tuck it behind her ear
Her shoulder bare with tilted clothes
She wears it without fear
She pulls one leg beneath the other
Comfort over propriety
She stifles a laugh, her mouth covered
Lost in what she reads
She turns the page and shuts her eyes
To think upon the story
At her own pace, she starts to rise
And makes her way right towards me
My heart stops, my stomach drops
My guilt and shame like sudden death
She smiles at me, greets, and nods
With my name in the same breath!

Being awestruck is not a bad thing, it's a *spectacular* thing.

Something done by someone has captivated you in such a way that you are forced to take the time and reflect on what just happened. Your reaction is so foreign to you that it has opened a new depth to your emotion. Your conclusions about what was possible are called into question. We all love to have our mind blown.

Furthermore, nothing quite measures up to the feeling that occurs when the subject of your awe actually **recognizes** you. This individual that has rocked your foundation, that seemed untouchable, has circled back and acknowledged your presence. Nothing else seems to matter in that moment. Whatever might have been eating away at you is overtaken by a feeling of euphoria that brings you happiness, confidence, and positivity. The source of awe could have come from infatuation, inspiration, devotion, or maybe just immense respect, but the underlying result is the same.

As amazing as it is, don't let it paralyze you. Don't let it be so overwhelming that it prevents your own **discovery** of how to reach their height. Don't let it lead you to dehumanize the subject of your awe. You will find that no matter how monumental the deeds, no matter how devout your feelings, they are still human. How are they to know you have been awestruck by them? Most likely, they look at themselves in a more critical light, and wouldn't imagine being untouchable. This needn't detract from the significance of their presence in your life, but should open the door to understand that not only *should* they be approached to further learn from them, but that they *want* to be approached.

On the other side of the coin, a person who has inspired awe in another should never take that for granted. What you've done is not amazing on its own. The unique pairing of what you've done and the individual it has influenced (whether it happened once or a million times over) is what is awe inspiring. Also know that it is infinitely easier for the subject of awe to initially approach the awestruck. Making yourself actively available to someone else will only compound the respect they have for you. Not only from a distance have you found a way to affect them, but up close and personal, you have proven you are imperfect just like them.

It may be desirable to keep the subject of your awe up on their pedestal and out of reach. To never sully the image that brings you inspiration. It will not be the truth, though. Fiction has its place and provides a medium for lessons that influence how we live, but we should seek out reality for what it truly is. Do not let the idea of someone from afar prevent you from understanding who they are up close. You may end up being disappointed, or pleasantly surprised, or awestruck anew. Regardless of the outcome, it will contribute to the understanding that extraordinary things are accomplished by ordinary people, and that nothing is preventing you from being a source of awe yourself.

Situational Questions

- Are you overwhelmed when in the presence of grandeur? Is it the lavish objects that hold your attention, or the people behind them? Are you in awe of the purchaser or the creator? Which one would you rather be?

- Do you shy away from approaching people that have come to mean something to you? If so, do you worry about what their reaction will be? What's the worst that could happen in genuinely expressing your feelings? If you're not shy, is the approach done without the expectation of something in return?

❧ Panic ❦

I stand right upon the edge
A perilous drop below
My heart it pounds outside my chest
My body has all but froze
I know the rope will hold my weight
I've seen it so many times
But what if it snaps, my bones will break
I need to control my mind!
The sweat is dripping down my neck
My vision seems impaired
Please just let me catch my breath
I'm really not that scared
Don't push me! I can do it myself
You'll make me slip and fall
They laugh as if I can't be helped
They know I'm trying to stall
What use for me to come out here
And leave without any fun
I shake my head to ignore the fear
And close my eyes and jump!

Panic sets in with the illusion of lost control.

When panic causes you to be **inactive** by conceding that there is nothing you can do, it prevents you from taking appropriate action within your control. Maybe the logical decision in the end *is* to do nothing at all, but it needs to be your decision, not a frozen reaction.

Panic can come about when something unexpectedly happens out of nowhere. If it is something immediately dangerous, you may curl up in fear. If it involves losing control over something important, you may be overwhelmed with the trouble that will ensue. In each case, a natural knee jerk reaction comes about that prevents you from using the faculties at your disposal. Your mind freezes and is unable to think through the situation. In a sense, you have caused yourself to be in **awe** of the adversity in such a way that it cripples you. But consider a different reaction: no reaction at all. Very little time is necessary to actually let the circumstances properly sink in, the most important part is that your mind remain fluid to allow it to happen. In that short amount of time, even a split second, you will be able to react in a logical manner. And often, not reacting at all, and letting the circumstances play out without any added **drama**, is a legitimate choice in the end.

Panic can also come about when something happens that you didn't *want* to happen. You may have prepared for its inevitability, but being confronted with the actual situation turns out to be a different matter altogether. Because it is *you* who has shown an aversion to it, consider the possibility there is no reason for panicking at all. Give the situation an opportunity to manifest your fears. Often, what you fear will not come about, and even if it does, you are still in charge of how you react.

Sometimes what you don't want to happen is the act of panicking itself, because you know you won't be able to control it. An interesting characteristic of this kind of panic is that it has no logical basis, and you *know* it has no logical basis. The influx of panic doesn't come about because you are scared of some object or situation, but because you are scared of the reaction you know you are going to have.

If you expect this kind of panic, you can combat its effects. If you've experienced true attacks of panic, you know that it is not reasonable to rely on your mind alone to steer you through it. It is too occupied with fending off the attack. I have found, however, that if you have something permanent to reference, you can anchor your actions upon it while still letting your mind finish its bout. Maybe this is a sheet of paper with your thoughts when speaking, or instructions to fall back on when carrying out a difficult task. By having these artifacts available to you, you are reinforcing your own control by deliberately moving the focus outside of your body. If you choose not to run from the panic, if you choose not to fight the panic, but rather ignore it and go about with what you need to accomplish, it will eventually fade away. Every time.

Situational Questions

- Do you worry about what other people will think when you take an action? Does this cause you to **doubt** whether you should go through with it? Do you have any proof that this reaction will occur? If you do have proof, what actual concrete harm will come to you if someone reacts poorly?

- In a pressure situation, have you made a mistake that has caused you to subsequently make more mistakes and lose control? Have you tried pausing, collecting yourself, and identifying the steps to reclaim control?

❧ Privacy ❧

This spotlight burns bright
Exposing every crevice of my wounds
Worse is the judging of your eyes
As I lay stark and ungroomed
The slightest whisper echoes round
My pain plain for all to hear
I cringe at its lonely sound
Softened only by my tears
I force myself to stand
And look up into the glare
I find shade behind my hand
And look down, my body bare
I feel ashamed of what I see
But all the same, it's who I am
If I don't care how I'm perceived
Why would the others give a damn?
I step outside the lighted oval
And am not scared if it will follow
I walk with purpose, ever hopeful
That I don't lose this strength tomorrow

Be open.

We are all human beings. We all make mistakes, we all have flaws, we all have aspects of ourselves we would rather keep hidden. When you can accept the reality that those characteristics you are afraid to expose will most likely be shared by someone else, it opens up a freedom to reveal who you are. A weight is lifted that no longer worries about what other people think, but only what you have accepted about yourself. Such honesty may open you up to more scrutiny than you desire, and leave you more vulnerable to attack, but putting up and maintaining walls that no one can assail is a full time job. When you let down your guard because you are comfortable with who you are, no energy is wasted. It becomes easy to calmly respond to attacks because you have left everything out on the table, and need only rely on the truth.

A contributor to wanting to maintain privacy is a false sense of **drama**. You may feel that aspects of your life are too *important* to be known by anyone else. That such information in the wrong hands could be catastrophic. Or, in a **superior** fashion, that others are simply not worthy of being privy to such details. There are certainly cases when precautions should be taken for private information, but each decision should be tempered with an understanding of the consequences of compromise, and the probability of it happening. When logic is overwhelmed with a paranoid attention to privacy, you will be prevented from focusing on more important things.

Conceding that you prefer to not reveal something is *still* being truthful. You needn't wander into the realm of **obscurity** to do so. Maliciously substituting private information with something dishonest takes it too far. Being caught in a web of lies is far more taxing, and damaging when the truth is revealed, than honestly withholding information.

Respecting the confidentiality of another individual is *still* being truthful. You are in charge of breaking the pattern of privacy for yourself, not violating someone else's right to it. By all means, urge the person who has confided in you to be honest about their secrets, but allow them to take that step for themselves.

Nobody is **perfect**. Privacy often comes about from a yearning to be **recognized** as perfect, for whatever reason. This, however, is a fruitless endeavor. Your outward appearance will most likely be regarded as artificial if it is centered around the idea of perfection. And is it not artificial? If you actively hide things about yourself so as to not taint the perception someone has of you, are you not fabricating an image that is not based on reality? Imperfection should be embraced, not covered in a shroud of privacy.

Situational Questions

- When you prepare for a display of knowledge, is it done with a worry of how you will be perceived? Do you not want the steps you took to reach your conclusions to be visible? If you allow yourself to make mistakes, and correct them in real time, are you not demonstrating a greater mastery of the subject?

- When creating something of value, do you feel you need to hide the strategies you employed to reach the finished product? Are you afraid of being overtaken by someone else who is inspired by those practices? Are you not confident enough in your own knowledge to best whatever else is created?

Personal Example

As I write this book, every modification turns into a new revision of the text. Most of it is terrible until I iterate on the idea. I would imagine most people do not like to put their unfiltered thoughts on display, and would rather the finished product be the only thing others see. My hope is, if there is enough interest, I will be able to share the entire revision history of this book from start to finish. I want people to learn from my mistakes and see my process. Forcing myself out of a defensive sense of privacy outweighs whatever unintended light the work might be seen in. We all go through the same pains, we just have to admit it, and should not be afraid to share it.

❧ Obscurity ❧

I lift my head up from the mud
Just enough so eyes can blink
I make sure no one sees my gun
As I rise onto the brink
My steps avoid these fallen leaves
Their crackles bring attention
My face disguised with dampened greens
That mask my real intention
The camouflage lets me blend in
And make my way unseen
But it fatigues my mind within
And weakens pressured knees
I grab a branch to bridge the gorge
Hand over hand with hands still wet
I slip and hurtle down with force
Plunging into shallow depths
I find my feet and stand up tall
The icy water cleansing weight
I thank the creek that broke my fall
And ripped this mask from my face

Be honest.

If **privacy** is the honest withholding of information, obscurity is the dishonest representation of it. For multitudes of reasons, we find it appropriate to mislead others because we think we will be, or they will be, better off. In its most innocent form, good intentions are blemished by white lies that may build up. In its most egregious form, someone is hiding who they truly are, or worse, they have convinced themselves they are something that they are not.

A monster who doesn't hide his face is preferred to a saint who has a mask on. It is in the abundance of truth and the absence of lies that love, support, respect, and loyalty should be sought out. When **validation** for any of these is chased in a fog of obscurity, their foundation is weakened. Only when someone fearlessly swims in the truth, and revels in the challenge of charting its waves, do they become a beacon of strength that can be relied upon.

Concealing pertinent information is warping the path for someone else's **discovery**. If you are the sole beneficiary of the action, it will invariably negatively affect someone else. Their conclusions will be tainted with falsehoods, their journey will be marred with misdirection. The benefit you receive is certainly outweighed by the detriment to them.

There are times when temporary obscurity benefits the entire group. There are certainly situations that are improved with tact and the timely release of information. One cannot be accused of selfishly hiding something if it is not meant to be a permanent fixture. However, if the cloak of obscurity is meant to never be lifted, it most likely descended for selfish reasons.

Obscurity can manifest itself through a sense of **helplessness**. It may seem to be the only way to survive a dishonest environment created by someone else. When the responsibility of truth is willfully ignored by others, it is easy to fall into the same pattern. In the end, however, the burden of falsehoods will be too much to bear. What originally might have been a reaction to having no other choice will morph into a web that cannot be escaped. The truth needs no justification, it needs no maintenance, it needs no support. It stands as a pillar on its own, and instead of being one you have to carry on your back, it is one you can lean on.

This book is not about judging evil ways and decrying malicious intent. It is about describing what we *naturally* do even when our intentions are good. With a benevolent goal in mind, it is often an acceptable compromise to obscure something as a means to achieve that goal. You may even consider it a display of strength that such resolve is needed to weather the **darkness** of your actions. But, like a fragile tower of cards, the slightest wind will topple the whole thing over. Is it a display of strength that you must depend on such fragility, or is it a reflection of the weakness of your intent?

Situational Questions

- How much time and energy do you spend on the maintenance of the obscurity you've created, or worry of being exposed? As time goes on, do you require further lies to keep the obscurity afloat? What other goals would you be able to focus on if the burden of dishonesty was lifted?

- What consequences would actually arise if the concealed information was revealed? Would it only negatively affect you? If so, are you unable to take responsibility for yourself? If not, have the others affected been given a choice in the matter?

❧ Inactivity ❦

I circle the mountain
My eyes to the stars
I think I can count them
If I try very hard
The peak to my right
Is so far away
It reaches the sky
I can't start today
These stars on the other hand
I can see right from here
Who else but me understands
How to keep them all clear?
I need to turn just a bit
For my count to continue
No time for me to sit
There's much for me to get through
After hours pass by
I am content enough to stop
I look behind me, oh my!
I've made it to the top!

Inertia is deadly.

It is easy to understand that getting *nothing* done is a bad thing, but even being *active* without an achievable goal or measurable progress is bad. In this sense, inactivity also describes the inability to change direction when needed. With goals in mind, actions should be taken with a purpose to work towards those ends.

To be clear, an action needn't be tedious or tiring for it to have a purpose. Rest is not inactivity, it recharges your body to press on. Play is not inactivity, it frees your mind to be creative. Entertainment is not inactivity, it exposes you to stories that can change your perspective. However, doing any of these things because there is nothing else to do, or because you are apprehensive about jumping into a daunting task, is an inactive choice. In a sea of stillness, avoiding active choices is quite appealing. It carries with it a **comfortable** burden of no responsibility, no sense of expediency, and no measure of accomplishment.

It is significantly easier to work through smaller tasks than spend an inordinate amount of time working through a larger task you've let sit and build up. You accumulate a debt of required activity if you procrastinate. From the start, if you wipe away that debt as it begins to rear its head, it is much easier to manage as time goes on. Even if you are behind, and the debt becomes monolithic, it can be broken down into manageable pieces to attack one at a time. It is never impossible, and should not be perpetually avoided.

Clean, condition, learn, toil: these are all verbs describing the elimination of some sort of debt. A debt of mess, a debt of weakness, a debt of ignorance, a debt of labor. It is probably the case you prefer some of these activities over others. If you can find a way to *combine* them, the debt may become more palatable. Some actions require you to actively think, and some do not. Someone who despises cleaning may find reprieve in simultaneously learning about something they enjoy. Someone who despises learning may find time passes more easily by also exercising. When one activity requires only the body, it can be offset by another that requires only the mind, or vice versa. In the end, it is all debt of activity that should be constantly chipped away at. The drudgery of doing something on its own can not only be balanced with something pleasing, but progress will be more efficiently made with both.

Continuing down this line of thought, when you are working your way through a task (desirable or not) that requires significant thought, you can often hit a roadblock of the mind that prevents you from progressing. Though you didn't decide for it to happen, you've naturally become inactive. If you run into this, stop what you're doing. Let the thoughts simmer while you preoccupy yourself with something else. Your subconscious mind is more equipped to grapple with such problems and you can come back to it refreshed. Having the agility to change gears on the fly and make the most out of your actions goes a long way in breaking the pattern of inactivity.

Situational Questions

- Are you shying away from a particularly monstrous task, almost feeling **helpless** in your approach to it? Have you considered breaking it into several smaller pieces that can each be accomplished in a single session? What if you charted out their details and measured your progress so the end is more visible?

- Are you mentally or physically exhausted from doing the same thing over and over? Is there an avenue for you to switch focus to something else? If you were able to take a break, would it be easier to get back in rhythm?

❧ Noise ❧

I stand here where the streets cross
In the busy of the day
I watch the bright lights lead off
The temporary race
My arms lift up to feel
The speed as it whisks by
I smell the burning steel
That rises to the sky
The honks and shouts and yells
Only bring with them distraction
I care not what he sells
I only look to find his passion
My words are never uttered
Unless they serve a need to learn
The noise flows to the gutter
While the truth it is discerned
I stand here as the night falls
And the city lays asleep
I listen for who might call
From the ever silent deep

Shut up and listen.

Every time you talk, you are taking away from your precious
time to listen.

Furthermore, when you consume information, *most* of it is going to be noise. More the reason your observational skills need to be honed to sift through what doesn't matter to find those few things that do matter. The **drama** of any perceived situation can be properly neutralized by targeting words, characteristics, and actions that are actually pertinent.

When every word has a purpose and meaning, more people are inclined to pay attention. When every foray into a conversation has an explicit intent, more people's ears will perk up when you begin to speak. By making a deliberate choice to not waste people's time, you are strengthening the power of your words. Any decoration around those words, whether it is being too verbose or showing flashing lights, only serves to distract.

An extra caveat in following this behavior, whether you find it positive or negative, is that it is *challenging*. It is very easy to vocalize every unfiltered thought that enters your brain, but training yourself to think carefully before you speak, and make sure each word surpasses your own threshold for importance, takes discipline.

Excessive noise can contribute to **blindness**. Awareness of your surroundings is hampered by a penchant for talking. The act of speaking naturally demands your full attention. There is very little else your mind is able to focus on as it summons words to describe your thoughts. In this sense, speaking is quite expensive, there are simply no more resources to absorb the rest of the details around you. If you are dedicated to continuing to learn, your words should be considered a precious commodity, as every use of them distracts you from taking in your surroundings.

Even when alone, noise can get in the way of your own thoughts. Through utter silence, you can better understand what is going through your mind. Meditation, however it may be practiced, eliminates the noise that you are generating yourself. This needn't take form through following an exercise that doesn't feel natural to you. In such a case, your fixation on the rules becomes noise in itself. Whatever natural method allows you to stop focusing on *anything* is more appropriate. It should make room for paced reflection of raw thoughts that you would otherwise overlook. In this space devoid of noise, you can come to terms with what really matters to you.

Situational Questions

- Do you find yourself worried that you will leave a conversation without making your point? Does that cause you to continue thinking out loud to make sure all your thoughts are fully covered? When someone else does this to you, do you tend to listen intently for the entirety of it? If you were to forget something, will your connection with that person be closed so abruptly such that you wouldn't be able to follow up if something else of importance came to mind?

- When you are communicating, how many other people's voices do you register? Are you agile enough to stop mid-sentence when a pertinent piece of information is brought up?

❧ Blame ❧

The structure collapsed
We stared in disbelief
Who exited last?
What time did you leave?
The foundation was sound
I checked it myself
It came to the ground
Thanks to someone else
It must be rebuilt
No matter the trouble
Absolved of my guilt
I walk to the rubble
I kneel at the scraps
And look close at the wreckage
I realize that the facts
Were not what I expected
I look back at my friends
This will hurt them the same
It starts to make sense
We share these burdened remains

Own your mistakes.

Don't shamefully and reluctantly *own up* to your mistakes, step up and actually *own* them. There's a misconception that it is somehow degrading to admit an imperfection. That it is more desirable to find blame in someone else and search for a way to justify your actions, no matter how erroneous they might have been. True confidence comes from being able to honestly reveal your own faults, not desperately try to conceal them.

Imagine every decision being made with a fear of failure. No risks would be taken, no ownership would be pursued, no sense of **discovery** would be had. Any creative environment must be safe to fail in. Good ideas should be scavenged from bad ones. Those good ideas would never have manifested if the bad ones weren't tried out. Successes bring temporary solace, but failures teach powerful lessons that shape your mindset. Failure shouldn't be feared, it should be embraced.

The use of the word failure above is describing something turning out worse than you expected or intended. You're never going to "blame" someone for a result that you wanted, you might even gratuitously take credit for it. Your reaction to a negative outcome, however, is much more telling. If you choose to ignore the lesson from a negative situation, you've truly failed. If you choose to pawn off responsibility when it really should be yours, you've truly failed. If you choose to complain because something didn't go your way, you've truly failed. You may not be able to control an outcome, but you absolutely can control your reaction to it.

If you are in a position of supervision, taking responsibility for the actions of those you supervise goes a long way. If someone feels they are not only being blamed, but they are being blamed by someone who is supposed to have an understanding of what they are doing, it can be demoralizing and frustrating. Blame that is **blind** to your own responsibility is the worst kind.

Outside of fleeting results that are undesired, there is a notion of chronically being in a situation you don't want to be in. As it seems to progress to a point of no return, and you feel **helpless** in changing it, it is natural to try to find blame in everything about it but yourself. It is easier to accept that the odds are stacked against you and that change is out of your control. Introspection in this case, truly figuring out what is within your control and what you're unnecessarily allowing to take control of you, will provide a path to breaking the cycle. The only thing standing in the way is yourself.

Situational Questions

- If someone *suggests* that you've done something wrong (even if in a **presumptuous** way), is your immediate reaction to find fault with someone else? How would your stress change if you took the time to investigate whether you made a mistake or not? If you are in error, do you try to conjure up justification for your actions?

- Do you stand to lose a great amount by taking responsibility for failure? Is your reaction to such hardship to impose punishment on yourself to set an example for others? Or do you take measures in the first place to be shielded from the consequences of your actions?

❧ Comfortability ❧

The soft caress of the clouds
Make my steps ever weightless
I gaze upon the earthly ground
And know that none can ever take this
I lose my balance and plummet
Soaked beads whipping my face
I find my feet at a summit
Seeming to come away unscathed
But under the rain and the hail
I feel pelts that leave bruises
I should be scared, but I fail
To take cover, the truth is
With my head lifted up
And my face numb with hurt
I cannot seem to get enough
But alas, I must return
As I lay once more on the cloud
Its caress nurtures my welting
I survey the lovely ground
And roll off for a fresh helping

Pleasure only comes from pain.

Remaining in comfort, no matter what way it manifests itself, will eventually lose its luster. Each experience will need to be topped with another more extravagant to surpass your rising standard of happiness. Only when you learn to strip away the comfort, and allow your mind and body to contend with hardship, will you appreciate relief when you come by it.

You are not challenging yourself if it doesn't result in being uncomfortable. A challenge being difficult for *most* other people does not mean it is a personal challenge. Conversely, one that is *easy* for most people can certainly be a personal challenge for some. Someone might be amazing at solving extremely complex problems, ones that most others cannot even comprehend, but effectively communicating it may leave them speechless. Someone may have a burning desire to find ways to overcome obstacles, but may dread the actual grind required to implement the solution. On the surface, a challenge may seem to be met, but the personal challenge is still being avoided.

When you get into a rhythm, it is natural to want to stick to situations that fit that rhythm. This is not to say that you should deliberately break it and lose your efficiency and expertise. But if the decisions you make are solely driven by the desire to **inactively** remain in a comfort zone, you are stymieing your ability to have new learning experiences. Especially when working in an environment with others, if you are taking strides to avoid the toil that others are going through, you won't be in a position to fully understand their situation. There is always a benefit in actively putting yourself in someone else's shoes, however uncomfortable they may be.

Aside from actual work, this pattern can also be applied to lifestyle. Dependency on luxury weakens you. If you are unable to function without the luxuries you've become accustomed to, you've crippled yourself. In a sense, you have locked yourself to a **formality** that you are unable to operate without. Worse, you've extinguished your ability to empathize with those who have no chance of experiencing that same luxury. The solution to this problem is always within reach. Whether it is small challenges throughout your day or sweeping changes to how you live your life, each choice is a substantial victory that continually makes you stronger.

Perpetual comfortability leaves you numb. When comfort has no discomfort or challenge to be compared to, its effect is diminished, if not eliminated altogether. You will be happier when you have something of worth to look forward to. The taste is sweeter when you're hungry, the reward is greater when you're challenged, the comfort is more appreciated when you're in pain.

Situation Questions

- How far do you go to push yourself to the limit? I don't mean constantly and without any rest, but when the opportunity arises, do you push yourself to the point of exhaustion of mind and body? Or do you do just enough so it is noticed?

- Are you afraid to exit the bubble you've become comfortable in? Is there a specific set of **dramatic** problems that repeat within that bubble? Do these consume the majority of your attention? If you were able to step outside and see what others are dealing with, would your problems gain more perspective?

❧ Obedience ❦

I join the rest in worship
Beneath this vaulted ceiling
My life who knows who chose it?
My dreams have lost their meaning
This wooden bench it creaks
As I shift my weight in despair
Again he starts to speak
Of how we're lucky to be here
The door why did they lock it?
I long to see outside
The key is in his pocket
I saw it with my eyes
The others' eyes are closed with bliss
I needn't wake them up
They found their peace in all of this
They fill this place with love
But the time has come to stand my ground
And pry that door right open
My fate is not to hang around
I'll die before I'm broken

Only *you* can know what you truly want.

Doing what someone else expects of you, when it goes against what you desire, is a great injustice. Your own happiness must take precedence over making someone else happy to your detriment. An expected adherence to **formalities** and traditions can shackle you from experiencing the world on your own terms. When attempting to break free, **doubt** may be introduced by those demanding obedience because their expectations have not been met, and their loyalty and sacrifice has not been reciprocated. If they are sincerely in your corner, however, and genuinely care for what you believe, they should be able to find happiness through their own actions, not yours.

In the case of creative and honest expression, obediently following standards that have been previously set, or complying with instructions in fear of reprisal, suppresses your own sense of originality and **discovery**. Do not allow your own voice to be lost. The unique way your mind works is *exactly* what needs to be displayed to the rest of the world. If you are in a situation that doesn't allow you to achieve this, and doesn't provide a path for you to eventually get there, seriously consider whether it is where you want to be.

This does not mean you should ignore rules that are placed in front of you. Do not misinterpret this pattern as an excuse to rebel in such a way that it is negatively affecting others. But in the fundamental cases of how you live your life, and what you are going to attempt to accomplish, only you can decide what is most important.

Those who habitually obey often do not recognize when they are undesirably asking for obedience. It may be the case that you have found happiness in following the path that was laid out for you. That is wonderful and it should be celebrated! In fact, you really weren't obeying at all because you came to terms with what you genuinely wanted for yourself. That path would've been discovered by you anyway. But when you ask something of someone else, think carefully whether you are doing so because it is *actually* right for them, or because it happens to fit your *interpretation* of what is right for them. Small things are inconsequential. In a caring relationship, someone will most likely be more than happy to indulge those requests, knowing what it means to you. But when this creeps into the realm of asking for a life change, you are stripping them of their independence and individuality. In the end, your relationship will be worsened because you are giving them legitimate reason to **resent** you. Unconditional support when it comes to letting someone blaze their own trail is powerful for a relationship.

Situational Questions

- Do you go to great lengths to assert your control over others? Is your influence so tenuous that it requires suppressing their freedom? If someone attempted to do this to you, what would your reaction be?

- Do you subscribe to the notion of the absoluteness of your path? That there is no possible other way to reach a fulfilling end? When you look at someone else who disagrees, do you consider them lost, regardless of the merits of what they've chosen for themselves?

❧ Desertion ❧

This land of sanded desert
Brings me such misery
I cannot stand the weather
I bake beneath the heat
I come upon a town of few
With morsels scattered on the ground
They're bitter when I try to chew
Can't force them to go down
I find a solitary well
Its foul liquid makes me choke
I feel I'm being dragged through hell
My grip it slips from hope
I crawl my way up one steep dune
And look on the horizon
Like magic came to give me proof
I walk towards a little island
Lush greens stud the oasis
I bend and dip my head in
A cool stream and drink to taste it
Like mana sent from heaven
I lay back after taking my fill
I wonder what if I missed it
If I hadn't had thought to climb that hill
I wouldn't have known that this existed

Don't dismiss something you didn't expect.

The most profound things we come across are those which we had no idea existed. If you give up on someone or something before you've fully experienced it, you may miss out on elements that surprise you. Often, this requires a thick skin. You need to be able to weather the offensive, the disgusting, the **boring**, the disappointing. If you are actually searching for these things, you must tolerate the opposite. If you habitually abandon that which you do not like, you will develop an aversion to more and more, causing your field of vision and experience to narrow. Painting anything with a general brush causes you to miss out on its hidden dimensions. Diamonds in the rough are not visibly out in the open, deep beneath is where the magic resides.

Aside from sitting back and absorbing an experience as a spectator, there is also the notion of intimately working together with someone to achieve an end. Desertion at this level can be devastating. In normal spontaneous conversation, a delicate dance ensues whereby alarm systems are up and topics do not venture into the uncomfortable. However, when someone is receiving instruction or feedback to maximize their performance, they must nakedly expose who they are, and a trust must be cultivated without any judgment. They are putting themselves on the line as they attempt something to the best of their ability. The smallest details of that interaction are registered, things you may normally not pay attention to. Any sense of **superiority** that emanates from you will cause them to shut down. Even silence is deadly: positive and constructive feedback should be instantly given. Furthermore, what *you* want needs to be communicated in such a way that *they* understand. If your goal is to bring out the best in this individual, it is incumbent upon you to translate your instructions to whatever is most aptly received by them.

The discussion above describes a temporary interaction, of which a positive outcome is desired by both individuals. One might also extend this pattern of desertion to a more permanent relationship, like having someone join a team for the long term. In your search for such a person, do not let your preconceived notions of what they should have already accomplished, or how they should act, cloud your judgment. If you solely look for a prototypical person that checks off the boxes on your list, you are limiting the number of people that can be of benefit to you. Furthermore, those prototypical people will have an erroneous assumption that *who they are* is more important than *what they can accomplish* when given the opportunity. When a wider net is cast, individuals will not take the opportunity for granted. Theorizing about what someone is capable of is no good. Allowing them to *prove* what they are capable of is better for both parties. Deserting those who do not fit the mold is counterproductive. Believing in someone and giving them a chance not only infuses them with confidence, but in the end can give you an asset that teaches you something you didn't know.

Every person has the potential in them to achieve greatness. If **capitulation** describes you giving up on yourself, desertion describes you giving up on someone else.

Situational Questions

- Have you conducted an interview in which someone didn't answer something the exact way you wanted? Did you dig deeper and try to figure out the substance of what they were trying to say, or did you give up on them immediately? In such a situation, are you more interested in asserting your own dominance, or exploring someone else's potential for growth? How far will you go to adapt your own viewpoint to discover the best in someone else?

- When attempting to teach something to someone, do you get frustrated if they are not on the same page as you? If they are having difficulty, is it a reflection of their inability to understand or your inability to present the information in a way that best serves them? As the master of such knowledge, is it not your responsibility, instead of the student's, to adapt?

- Is there a particular genre or form of entertainment that you scoff at? Have you taken the time to listen to a fan of it explain why they like it? Have you tried honestly experiencing it for yourself, all the way through, and giving it an unbiased chance?

∾ Capitulation ∾

My boots leave holes beneath the snow
They reach up to my knees
A trodden path I keep in tow
Should I ever choose to leave
Colossal trees seem to rise
To heights that have no end
Their sodden oak feels so dry
Immune to moisture's bend
Thickening fog makes me pause
And squint to find my bearing
I am distraught to be lost
The voice within is staring
The step behind calls my name
And beckons me to look back
The step in front has not been made
And is silent without a hand
This forest is enclosing me in
So much safer if I left it
But just as I chose to begin
I walk on to find the exit

It's not that you can't do it, it's that you won't do it.

Solving a problem requires persistence, not innate ability. If
you simply choose to spend more time, the solution to a
problem will eventually surface. If you give up before you

have had the chance to see progress, not only will you miss out on the solution, but you will mistakenly be under the impression you are incapable of discovering it. Do not let **helplessness** in the face of difficulty cause you to give up.

Mastering something requires practice, not predisposition. There is no difficulty in the act of practicing, the process itself is very straightforward: simple repetition. The only hurdle in the way is your own dread of committing so much time to it. If mastery is your ultimate goal, there is no problem left to solve, only a choice to make. This does not mean you should narrowly focus on one goal without reevaluating if it has the same priority for you as it did before. It is legitimate to shift focus to something you truly desire instead of continuing to go down a path you will eventually regret.

There is a misconception that you need to be born with a penchant for learning in order to be successful. Genius is not an abnormal capacity to learn, it is an abnormal hunger to learn. The only thing standing in your way of achieving something is yourself. If you concede before you even start that you are not capable of doing it, you've already lost.

There are some very specific things that require an innate physical or artistic talent, things that simply cannot be trained. If that born talent is there, the only obstacle left is your own desire to work harder than anyone else. If that talent is not there, which for most of us is the case, that leaves everything else in this world to choose from. All you have to do is pick. When it comes to actually receiving an opportunity to be formally trained for such a skill, or compensated, or join a team of like minded individuals, we may not always be **recognized**. But that isn't the reason you should be doing it in the first place. The commitment to practice and work harder than anyone else is exclusively within your control. There are simply too many learning resources at your disposal for there to be any excuse that something cannot be learned, practiced, and mastered on your own.

Every challenge should be met with the certainty that not only *can* it be overcome, but it *will* be overcome. It may require tackling it one step at a time, it may require shifting priorities in other areas. Capitulation at any point is not an indication that the challenge has become insurmountable, but that you've chosen to give up.

Situational Questions

- If you have chosen to change the direction of your goals, are you doing it on your own terms? Or is it in reaction to a setback that has made it feel too difficult? Are you falling back to a more **comfortable** state?

- When confronted with a problem, do you get angry with yourself because a solution is not immediately apparent? Have you considered stepping away, letting it simmer in the back of your mind as you attack other tasks, and then coming back to it? Have you tried getting input from people you trust?

❧ Perfection ❧

This piece will be a masterpiece
Anything less would be worthless
Perfection, it has to be
Anything else, and I will burn it
Every stroke will be deliberate
Braided with the touch of an expert
I cannot hope to ever live with
The slightest flaw will be remembered
When they lay eyes on my work
They will tremble with envy
In every corner there will lurk
Another reason to commend me
But as I paint with steady hand and
See the strain of what's expected
I cannot play without abandon
I am not free to be reckless
Let me snap in half this canvas
And wipe the tainted slate clean
I am foolish to have demanded
The unblemished and impossible gleam

Perfection is both unattainable and undesirable.

Perfection is subjective. What one person sees as a strength another might see as a flaw. You, or your work, will never be loved by *everyone*. You, or your work, will never be hated by *everyone.* It is impossible for someone or something to be comprehensively accepted or looked at in the way it was intended. No matter how long you toil to make something *just* right, it will be a fruitless endeavor in the eyes of someone. For this reason alone, perfection is unattainable.

Now, let's hypothetically say there actually was some way to reach perfection. Would it even be desired? The more success, the more **recognition**, the more admiration someone has, the more people will want to bring them down. The more people will actively search for flaws they can expose and exploit. Why is that? Why would perfection not be celebrated all around? When you are humanized, through mistakes and characteristics you acknowledge and accept, your journey is something others can imagine themselves taking. They do not **resent** you for having something they cannot attain, because you also have something they want to avoid. If your underlying goal is to bring out the best in others, and help them achieve great things, it cannot be done from a perch of **superior** perfection.

A work of art is never finished, it is merely abandoned. An artist, and I mean this to include any individual who attempts to *create* anything, will always be able to find something they want to change. If given all of eternity, they will perpetually be able to tweak or redo a work, each iteration being more perfect than the last. If you get caught in this endless cycle, you will have achieved *nothing.* You will waste time such that nothing can be completed, and you strangle your ability to explore the rest of your prowess. At some point, that work needs to be shared with others. Don't let fear of someone else not **validating** your work prevent you from finding a stopping point. Complete something that reasonably reaches your standards, receive actionable criticism, and iterate until it reaches your newly modified standards. Then, this is the most important point, *move on*. Something must be abandoned for you to shift focus onto a new undertaking, and continue to learn. Eternally grasping for perfection is a waste of time.

A final point about receiving criticism from others. If you are so invested in the idea of being perfect in some aspect of your life, you are setting yourself up for disappointment when someone comes along and contests it. And this *absolutely* is going to happen. Be comfortable with what you have accomplished, and what it means to *you*. Have a thick skin and be able to take criticism with a grain of salt. Don't let your happiness be predicated on being perceived as perfect, because it can never be achieved.

Situational Questions

- When attempting to master something, do you strictly adhere to the teachings presented to you? Do you berate yourself when the slightest detail is missed? In your quest for mastery, have you made room for exploring on your own and creating something new? Where is *your* identity shown?

- Are you so critical of your own work that you end up hating anything you finish? Have you allowed others to supply their opinion about it? If it is positive, is there a reasonable compromise between your own negativity and their support? If it is negative, are you taking actionable steps to improve the quality?

Personal Example

This book is extremely important to me. In my mind, writing it is the most significant thing I've attempted. That weight comes with a natural fear of it not ending up *perfect*. I wish for all my thoughts to be so flawlessly laid out that they never need improving. This, however, is simply not possible. I will always be able to find something I want to change if given enough time. Not only does it make sense to update these thoughts as I gain new experiences, but the door will always be open to continue communicating them. There will invariably be mistakes that I want to correct, but I need to *finish* at some point.

❧ Drama ❧

"This crown it tilts atop my head
I think I'll need a new one
This sapphire has a tinge of red
I said I want a blue one
Ah, I look so dreadful in this dress
Where is that wretched little seamstress?
She'll yield to me a pound of flesh
No room for an ounce of weakness
You there! What's your name again?
Pick that up from the floor!
If you ever drop my train again—
Who is that knocking at the door?"
"Ma'am I loathe to bring these tidings
But I've been asked to be the martyr
The prince has gone in hiding
Stricken with cold feet at the altar
He asked to give this rose
Please forgive me for the hassle
But since the prince is indisposed
I must escort you from the castle."

Focus on the very *little* that is actually important.

Important things should vastly outweigh unimportant things, yet the latter seems to vastly *outnumber* the former. When disproportionate weight is given to these unimportant things, everything starts to look critically important. Soon, the fact that there are so many problems becomes a critical problem in itself. The actual significant facts about a situation become diluted, and are difficult to fish out from the sea of drama you have engulfed yourself in.

What is actually important? One measurement is how *chronic* the problem is. If the problem is permanent, or at least frequent, it's reasonable to attach importance to it. If attention is not paid to temporary problems, time alone will take care of their existence. If priority is given to less frequent problems, energy is being wasted. This doesn't mean they should completely fall off the radar, but drama should be judiciously given to those problems where when a solution is applied, the greatest benefit will come about. Be careful not to use this threshold as an excuse to deliberately avoid something you don't want to confront; letting it fester will only make it worse. But when your initial reaction is to rush to judgment, think about how chronic the problem is, and whether or not your energy is best spent on it.

Another effective approach is to filter out problems that *only* affect you. We have a tendency to attract attention to the things we feel others are not aware of, and unfortunately the subject is often ourselves. When your own well being, or your own way of thinking, is exclusively being taken into consideration, the importance of the problem diminishes greatly. Important things tend to affect many people, and if the solution to the problem will lead to a positive outcome for all, it is worth paying attention to.

A fair criticism of this line of thought would be that people who *do* blow things out of proportion will always be able to get their way. To be clear, you *should not* be a push over. When it matters, you absolutely need to push back. You will find, however, that if you take the time to filter out the nonsense, there is very little you have to expend your energy on, and it can be honed and concentrated for those few important situations. So what if others are winning the small, unimportant battles? Their time and energy is being wasted, and when they are confronted with an important problem, they will be ill equipped to handle it. You, on the other hand, will have been waiting for such a moment, and will have a fresh and uninhibited mind to attack it.

Finally, though the focus so far has been on problems, achievements are also prone to have drama creep up on them. Just as a problem can bring about unnecessary **panic**, an achievement can lead to unnecessary grandeur. This is less severe, since feeling overwhelmed with problems is much more damaging than feeling overwhelmed with glory, but maintaining humility concerning an achievement goes a long way. It should be enough that *you* are aware of what it means to you. Let someone else unselfishly provide the drama for it, if there is reason to do so.

Situational Questions

- Do you find yourself interrupting other people? Is it that you feel you need to be heard, in which case, are you just adding **noise**? Is it that you feel you have something more important to say, in which case, are you unwittingly **blind** to the importance of what is already being said?

- When you ask something of someone, or celebrate an accomplishment, do you use the term "I" or "we"? If you use the term "I", are you feeling an extra sense of drama with what you are saying? If you use the term "we", is it tempered with the realization that you share the responsibility with others?

❧ Validation ❦

This shield that I've crafted
Will withstand all attack
Its design has everlasted
All the objections I have had
I needn't take it into battle
Lest it lose its lovely charm
Don't you agree? It can't be rattled
Though it would remove you from harm
Why do you unsheathe your sword?
You put me on the defense
You swing at me? Good lord!
My shield splinters and dents
You swing again, you're mad!
My shield crumbles to the floor
And yet again, I'm glad
You have humbled me once more
I will clean up this mess
And build another more resilient
Sharpen that sword, and rest
I will require its brilliance

Let it break.

If you are able to defend your belief against an opposing argument, that belief will only become stronger. If you are only seeking viewpoints that validate your beliefs, they will inherently be weak. When such tenuous conclusions form the basis of action, they will inevitably fall apart against the slightest of challenges. To compensate, you might find yourself resorting to **obscurity** in order to prevent unwanted scrutiny. Conclusions should not be molded to achieve a predetermined end, they should be beacons guiding us to the correct ends.

Debate is the cornerstone of making sure good ideas are the best ideas. Only when there is a genuine desire for improvement, on both sides, is debate worthwhile. Otherwise, it is simply two precalculated narratives trying to outsell each other. Humility should be present, dissent should be welcomed, and **formality** should be thrown away. In this arena of unfiltered thought, where no suggestion is too absurd to be considered and no question is naive enough for ridicule, a competition of minds breeds the strongest of ideas.

Clinging to a belief exposes you emotionally to it, especially when it is a fragile one. When it is finally debunked, you may be devastated and lose the confidence to continue. This behavior causes you to seek validation in order to protect your innocence. Your primary motive should *always* be to seek the truth; allow yourself to be emotionally attached to *that* goal. If you uncover a lie then you will be infused with a vigor and passion to find the truth behind it.

When forming a conclusion, it must be tested. That test can come from debate, or from a more scientific approach that can give you measurable results. In either case, do not go into a test looking for confirmation. There has to be an open mind that you could be wrong, and an actual *desire* to know that you *are* wrong as soon as possible. The quicker you know that a conclusion is false, the quicker you can abandon it and move on to another with more merit. If you are genuinely trying to reach a verifiable conclusion, it is tragic to unknowingly and unnecessarily believe in a false one. Seek out dissent and reinforce conclusions by testing them in unfamiliar waters. A healthy skepticism about assumptions provides fertile ground for not only spotting, but pulling out weeds.

It is very easy to validate someone else's opinion, or work, or decisions. There is quick gratitude and reward in doing so. It is much more difficult to sincerely question it, with the motivation of improving it in the long run for their own benefit. When your own ambition obscures your desire to positively influence someone else, you will carry the guilt of taking advantage of weakness. Forging a relationship where honesty and candor is reciprocated will strengthen your resolve.

Situational Questions

- Do you make broad generalizations of what is going on in someone else's head? Does this practice serve to fuel a narrative of who they are or how they go about things? Have you actually bothered to ask them? Who benefits from such a narrative?

- When an outcome arises or evidence is presented that contradicts you, do you concede that you were wrong? Or do you try to warp your initial viewpoint to give the perception of being right? What is more important to you, a facade of correctness, or a confidence in weathering flaws in judgment?

❧ Doubt ❧

My hand it clenches on this door knob
The bag I've packed around my shoulder
It still is nice inside this warm loft
The wind outside it seems much colder
He says he loves me more than life
That he can't live without me present
But then I must bring out the knife
When he starts to lose his senses
My eye was blackened with his reach
And I chose to take no more
Though his touch is soft, his voice is sweet
When I get up from the floor
His temper rages with a snap
I never see it coming
He says I won't be hard to track
If I ever think of running
I crack the door with just a sliver
To breath in the chilly air
And though my body starts to quiver
I know I must go anywhere but here

When you make a decision, and circumstances have not changed, stick to it.

Your decisions should not be influenced by unsolicited opinions of others. It may be the case that you require *information* from others to help reach a decision, but any *opinion* should be taken with a grain of salt. In the end, it is your vision and your own instinct that must be followed.

Doubt can often arise when choosing to leave a situation of **comfort**. The uncertainty of the new environment is weighed against the consistency of what you are accustomed to. But, there must be a reason that caused you to come to the choice in the first place. That reason doesn't change, the circumstances leading to that reason often do not change, only your own doubt begins to creep in. Do not let your focus be taken off the goal you have laid out for yourself. Additionally, you may even feel a sense of loyalty or obligation to the people that share or helped create those comfortable surroundings. That loyalty needn't diminish, and it will most likely be reciprocated with an encouragement to follow your desires. If not, and you are vilified for your choice, you must ask whether their selfish demand for **obedience** should be a cause for renewing your doubt, or eliminating it altogether.

Doubt is easy. It takes no effort to second guess yourself, but it takes great strength to stay focused on an achievable goal and not let anything outside of that goal sway you. Threats, promises, **panic** all tug at a decision every which way in hopes of taking your eye off the *goal* the decision is meant to achieve.

This goal must be a clear and honest one. Breaking the pattern of doubt should not translate into a stubbornness that prevents you from being agile. You must be able to steer your decision in a better trajectory towards the goal. If your decision was based on particular information, and that information has changed, then the decision should be carefully and deliberately reviewed.

Sifting through what might be a mountain of information can be difficult. Know that your decision was based on very *few* things, like your end goal and aspects of your circumstances related to that goal. Doubt is often introduced when there is an erroneous focus on extra information that didn't even have a bearing on the original decision. When the source of doubt is another person, they tend to focus on information *they* have control over. When an honest decision is made, it is normally based on information the *decision maker* has control over.

Situational Questions

- Do you feel the step you're going to take might be the wrong one? If so, so what? When you look back, will you regret having stepped forward and taken a chance, or will you regret having stood still in wonder? What will cut deeper, the infinite expanse of what could have been, or the certainty of what did occur?

- Have you been given an ultimatum from a person that forces you to choose between them and someone else? Is that other person giving you the same ultimatum? If not, would you rather maintain a relationship with someone who made you choose, or one who understood you enough to give you freedom?

❧ Presumption ❧

The beast towered above the men
Whose pitchforks prodded in outrage
It viciously growled in order to send
Them back to where crowds came
The child was stuck atop the tree
They couldn't abandon their young
Wielding torches, they yelled and screamed
Flames flickered from every tongue
The beast dropped back to shield its face
Then stared at the boy cornered
Its monstrous paw lifted and raised
The villagers gasped in horror
With a smile and squeal of delight
The child leaped on to the hand
With virtuous care, gentle and light
The beast kneeled down to the land
He ran to his father standing speechless
The beast exhaled a knowing sigh
It slowly rose up and turned to leave them
Quietly stomping into the night

Don't jump to conclusions.

Expect the worst in someone and you will most likely receive
it. You have already made a judgment about how they are
going to act, so why should they go through the trouble of

proving you wrong? Expect the best in someone, however, and that faith will be received with humility. The individual is more likely to want to prove that they can live up to that positive image. Note that this faith is not the same as encouragement. Vacuous words telling someone to give it their best shot is quite different from *actually believing* that they will be able to step up to the challenge. The difference is palpable, and will be felt by the recipient.

When someone has done something wrong, or incorrectly, or bad, or negative in any way, approaching them with the presumption that it was deliberate will be received with spite. In addition, their response will be to reciprocate by actively searching for your mistakes and vilifying you for them. You have approached them with condescension, and a connotation that you would never do such a thing. On the other hand, if the benefit of the doubt is given, the response will be much more positive. If you presume they probably made a mistake, that you recognize it was an innocent mistake, and that you could've made the same mistake yourself, it will be received with an eagerness to correct it and a willingness to forgive you when it happens to you. And it will happen to you.

Prematurely jumping to conclusions can also backfire. It may be the case that what you perceived as a mistake was not a mistake at all. You were missing important information that in the end made *you* look like a fool. It is easy to immediately seek **validation** for **blame** in someone else. It is more prudent to take a step back, discover the facts in a way that is not intrusive or arrogant, and make sure you are reaching the right conclusion.

This point about arrogance is an interesting one to explore. A sense of **superiority** underlies an initial negative assumption about someone else. A sense of **perfection** underlies a *lack* of any negative assumption about your *own* self. Both stem from a desire to be **recognized** as such. When you can rid yourself of this preoccupation, and focus on how you are able to bring out the best in a person through an interaction, you will find much greater reward. Entering it with arrogance will only serve as a seed for **resentment**, and will counteract the positive way you wish to be perceived. Be humble enough to be proven wrong, and gentle enough to prove you're right.

Situational Questions

- If you come across someone who fits a physical stereotype, do you expect them to act in accordance with that stereotype? What if you flipped your reaction and expected them *not* to validate the stereotype? How might your interaction with them be different?

- When given a piece of information, does your mind wander to the worst consequences of it? Are you able to wait for all the facts to be available before reacting? Do you let others' interpretations influence yours, or can you trust in your own ability to extract the truth?

❧ Resentment ❧

I pace around locked in this cage
The bars they leave me frightened
I throw myself against them enraged
My straight jacket seems to tighten
Your voice is all I hear in my head
It rings with condescension
You hope I end up lying here dead
To bring you towards ascension
I collapse with exhaustion
As my screams wither in vain
I think of how I was lost when
You slowly creeped in my brain
Did you even want to be there?
I feel the jacket loosen
Did you know I thought it unfair?
My arms unwrap with movement
Whether your answer gives me peace
Or just crowds me with more fear
Forgiveness is all I have within reach
I look up, the bars they've disappeared

Let it go.

When you begin to resent someone, every word that comes
out of their mouth, every action they take is overly
scrutinized and interpreted as an amplification of what you

resent them for. It consumes you to such a point that you have relinquished control of your thoughts to them. You feel that if nobody else is actively acknowledging their faults, your time is best spent venting to yourself. Your own internal anger is an unavoidable consequence of the necessary, perpetual spite. All the while, they could not care less what you think.

You do not have control over the actions of who you resent. You cannot let your happiness be defined by whether the person stops what they are doing or gets what's coming to them. You will be waiting for an outcome that you are unable to influence, or worse, waste time and energy attempting to fruitlessly change the situation.

Consider the possibility you are being **presumptuous** of their actions. If you can assume it is not deliberate, that it is simply an unconscious characteristic they aren't even aware of, it will open the door for you to see the good qualities in them. If that assumption is unfounded, and what they are doing actually *is* deliberate and malicious, then you should pity them for needing to compromise their integrity. Furthermore, the individual you resent may actually be quite talented and intelligent, despite these characteristics. In that case, use the opportunity to learn from them, even it if must be done in a calculated way to minimize your resentment. Do not let hatred cut off a valuable learning resource.

Even with someone you haven't met personally, you may feel jealousy or envy from afar. Maybe they have received accolades you feel are undeserved. Maybe they have accomplished something you wish *you* had the opportunity to. The potency of their **recognition** will certainly be intense for it to have traveled such a great distance to your life. In any case, you are fixated on things that are outside of your control. Every resentful second you spend brooding is a second you are taking away from achieving your own goals. Instead of longing for what they have, take steps to make it a reality for yourself.

The ultimate salvation from resentment is forgiveness. Do not, however, approach forgiveness as an unselfish act. Yes, forgiving someone, whether they deserve it or not, may have the consequence of absolving them of their guilt. But the freedom you receive from no longer holding that grudge greatly outweighs whatever advantage comes to the accused. Their name, their voice, their presence will no longer spark negative emotion. Such liberation is priceless.

Situational Questions

- Are you scrutinizing the actions of the person you resent more than others? Imagine someone you *like* taking the same action, would it still bother you? Would you be more likely to ignore it if it came from them?

- Do you worry that other people are not recognizing the same faults you see? What are the actual consequences of them not being aware? If there are consequences, have you spoken your mind to those it would affect, and left it for them to deal with?

- Do you find yourself only happy when something negative happens to this person? So happy that you wait for and savor in those moments? Do you have any control over such events?

❧ Helplessness ❧

Chains around my wrist and neck
Chains between my ankles
They ask for me to show respect
And they will show they're thankful
"Just tell us some of what you've heard
We don't even need it all."
The whip slides on the uneven dirt
And lifts up from its crawl
The lash comes down across my chest
Stinging loud amid my silence
Pleas come from my pulsing flesh
To end the stream of violence
My bones may break in pieces
But my soul remains intact
My choice may leave me grievous
But control it slips their grasp
They grab my hair and beg me, "Please
Don't make me keep this pace."
I laugh under a weakened wheeze
And spit blood in their face

You always have a choice. Always.

In the best of situations, your confidence and freedom to follow your heart has no obstacles. In the worst of situations, you feel trapped in **obedience** and unable to break free of your physical circumstances. You may even feel crippled with your own trepidation of taking the first step.

When faced with daunting circumstances, there is a tendency to wait for a random window of opportunity to surface. Doing everything within your power to make the most of it when it comes along is certainly wise, but don't allow it to be the only shepherd of your happiness. Only that which is in your control can be relied upon. Anyone successful will have seized their lucky break, but the lack of such a break will not cause them to feel trapped. Helplessness is not a mountain of factors against you or an absence of factors aiding you, it is a **capitulation** and false concession that you cannot help yourself.

Even if your immediate personal situation is acceptable, the machinations around you may feel out of your control. The powerful apparatus you cannot take apart, the historical establishment you cannot penetrate, the inner workings of the cabal you cannot witness. The worst response to such a situation is **inactivity**, going with the flow because there is nothing else that can be done. Understand that change starts by simply making a choice. How you choose to live your life in the shadows of dire circumstances speaks greater volumes than even the most persuasive of voices. Instead of hoping that someone comes along to reform a process, cease to support anyone who goes along with it. Instead of waiting for the status quo to come around to your way of thinking, reject its effect on your life. Know that you are never alone in these choices. You may not have met them, you may never meet them, but such choices will inevitably resonate with someone else, and they will follow suit. It is through the cascading effect of choices, not talk, that culture is forced to bend to the will of the majority.

The power of choice is monumental. It can describe the insignificant things that matter to you. It can describe whether you are willing to die for what you believe in. It is a power that can absolutely, unequivocally, under no circumstance be ever taken from you. This life is a temporary one, and what you do with the time you have will either cause you to look back with regret or satisfaction. Letting your choices succumb to a feeling of helplessness will ultimately leave you with regret. Whatever choice you make will certainly have consequences and repercussions, but the choice is always yours.

Situational Questions

- Do you feel beholden to your current circumstances, however problematic, because of the financial stability it provides? What are you doing with the spare moments, however sparse, you have to yourself? Are you *thinking* about what it would be like step away, or are you slowly taking steps, however small, to get it done?

- When you are forced into a less than ideal situation, do you spend time pining about where you wish you were? Have you given your current situation its full due? If you have, what can turn your dreaming into action?

❧ Superiority ❧

The wine was delicately poured
They dined in extravagance
The wives were subtly ignored
He didn't want them mad again
"I've been endowed with many gifts,"
He quipped while straightening his tie,
"I love the sound when money flips
My skills are more than you require."
"Then let me pose another question,"
The other said with eyebrows raised
His fingers closed behind his neck then,
"Tell me, how much are you paid?"
"One hundred strong, quite a prize
A hefty sum in just a year!"
By then the lady rolled her eyes,
"Your math is very off, my dear
Full forty for a mansion
Empty to the brim
Twenty for the second car
Never taken for a spin
Three for the suit you wear
Of which you have nine others
Three fourths of what is left to spare
So we don't die from hunger
Leaving two and fifty in the bank
As if we've been robbed!"
"Sir I think you have your wife to thank
I'm giving her the job."

You're not better than me. I'm not better than you.

No matter who you interact with, you will always be able to learn something from them, and they will always be able to learn something from you. A sense of superiority, on either side, is not only demeaning, but prevents the offender from being able to grow. If you have the preconceived notion that you are somehow above another, you've constructed an artificial barrier to new learning experiences.

An interesting thing about superiority is that it only exists relative to someone else. When you try to be the *best*, and that is the only thing important to you, the goal is being restricted to the accomplishments of others. Your measure of success is based on being **recognized** in a superior way to someone else. If you can rid yourself of the need for recognition, and focus on approaching each interaction with a desire to come out better than you entered, you will open up new avenues of maturation that you wouldn't have otherwise been aware of.

This is not to say you shouldn't strive to be outstanding at what you do. Challenging yourself, getting out of your comfort zone, and attacking your goals are all admirable qualities. However, they don't have to be worn on your sleeve and advertised to every person you meet. If you have a genuine desire to bring out the best in the people around you, and continue to learn from them, your natural tendency to want to show off your talents needs to be restrained. By all means, share your successes with those who are close to you, who are past the point of being potentially insulted or taking something the wrong way. But approaching each new acquaintance with a sense of equality and eagerness to learn will go a long way.

Even after reading all this, you may still be convinced that you really *are* superior to others, but you agree it may be prudent to hold that feeling back. If this is the case, consider this: during your life, you probably have been presented with amazing and lucky opportunities that you've been fortunate enough to seize and make the most out of. Your initial success might have given you the confidence to expand what you are capable of. Your support network may have given you the encouragement to persevere through difficult times. The point is that nobody gets to where they are *all by themselves*. Ever. If you can come to this realization, it is the first step to understanding that your sense of individual superiority has ironically been justified by things outside of your control, things that you didn't make happen on your own. This humility can lead to much more rewarding experiences with others.

Situational Questions

- When you meet someone new, do you have an initial reaction about what class they fall into relative to you (for example by profession, wealth, ancestry or geography)? What if you entered that meeting with a genuine belief that you are both equals?

- Imagine there was nobody left to show off to, would you still take the time to quantify your greatness? Would there be any more reason to **dramatize** your achievements?

✤ Darkness ✤

I row across this pool of blood
Faces screaming in the boils
My ears start ringing from the flood
Of haunting voices, I recoil
I try to find deliverance
But the raucous current overtakes me
Drenched with sin, my body's fallen in
I gasp the noxious air and look for safety
Skeletons upon the shore
Pierced with mirrors of their crimes
Every step I take shatters more
Their cracks run up my spine
I see reprieve in a narrow ray
That shines with golden splendor
Dripping, I crawl and drag my way
Then stop, wounds swollen tender
If I climb up to the light
The demons' slightest touch will corrupt
But if I stay down here and fight
I will never come undone

You cannot control what you think, you *can* control what you do.

You may have convinced yourself that, at the very least, your *mind* is **perfect**. Though you have made mistakes in the past, those circumstances were not a result of any corruption of the soul. Your mind has been purged of any dark thoughts, and you find it deplorable to think of anything impure. With this mindset, however, the dark thoughts that *do* unconsciously crawl into your psyche (and they absolutely will) will be mistakenly accepted as appropriate, and reasonable to be acted upon. You know you can do no wrong, correct? If the thought has made it past your impenetrable defenses, surely there is merit to it. When you attempt to justify everything that goes through your mind, you lose the ability to separate the good from the bad.

It is not a foreign concept that the exact thing you try to avoid thinking about becomes your fixation. The irony of not accepting your own darkness is that you are causing yourself to be haunted by it. You are putting yourself in a position to be more easily overcome, the opposite of what you intended. It is a much more prudent exercise to embrace the things about your mind that you are scared of. Acknowledge it, never ignore it, and make a clear distinction between your thoughts and your actions. The full repertoire of your knowledge and reasoning will act as a natural filter that prevents your actions from being the wrong ones.

We are all insane. We may choose to filter what we present to the world, but in the end, we are all insane. There are deranged thoughts going through our heads that scare us, that we know will scare someone else if we share them. Keeping this insanity **private**, however, only serves as a mechanism to ostracize the things that shock us. An environment that places a taboo on vocalizing and depicting things that are vulgar, obscene, or contemptible is obstructing our ability to gain more knowledge. It cripples our ability to be resilient and defend against their effects. But if the culture we surround ourselves in can make the distinction between *thought* and *action*, our conversations will be more open, honest, and worthwhile. The righteous crusader who attempts to eliminate evil focuses his attention on preventing negative action, not thought. Indeed, the *act* of preventing *thought* is a dark one in itself.

If you are to accept that there is a negative characteristic that should be avoided for each pattern laid out in this book, the strategy for doing so should *not* be to try to eliminate them from your mind. It is natural to think about falling into one of these patterns. If this is acknowledged, then you can train yourself to not let those thoughts translate into actual negative actions. Embrace what you fear you will do, and make an active choice to not do it.

Situational Questions

- Can you play the character of something that scares you? Can you let go of inhibition and lose yourself in the role? This needn't be done in front of someone else, that is a different matter altogether. But in your own skin, are you comfortable enough to own another persona and see where it takes you?

- Do you get nervous when you hear or see something that you believe is wrong? Does that reaction make you more susceptible to its effects? Are you equipped and confident enough to confront it?

❧ Recognition ❧

On this island alone
Without a chance to escape
I silently roam
Quietly losing my faith
But when the sun blazes
I don't look for the shade
And when the wind chases
I stare it square in the face
My discipline strengthens
With no reliance
I live with a vengeance
In pure defiance
But the temperature drops
My body cannot survive
I will not let my heart stop
Until it hardens to ice
I lay here in this final hour
Frozen, time still forever
No one will ever know of my power
But I... I will remember

Do it for yourself.

If nobody is looking, if nobody is aware of who you are or what you are doing, what exactly will you do? If nobody is there to give you accolades, or give you encouragement, or fire you up with criticism, or hand you a reward, with what resolve will you get it done? Every second you wait for recognition is a second wasted. Welcome it when it comes, but have a clear path going forward without it. The only person you *ever* have to prove something to is yourself.

Recognition comes in many forms: payment, victory, success, adoration. When these ends become your sole focus, you lose sight of what actually means something to you, what lasts. If I am given money I haven't earned, I don't want it. If I have to cheat to win, I don't want it. If it is handed to me on a silver platter, I don't want it. If I am offered credit for something I didn't do, I don't want it. If I have to choose between going up against the best and losing or going up against the worst and winning, I would rather lose because I know I will have pushed myself to the limit. The outcomes of these trials pale in comparison to our own understanding of what we went through to get there. We may not be able to convince others of this struggle, but in the end, it is our own knowledge that truly matters.

All of the end goals mentioned above come through in copious amounts when they are the least of your worries. It is *specifically* your own desire to achieve what you want, regardless of recognition, that will resonate with others. Conversely, if that desire is fake and **obscures** a more artificial purpose, the uncovered truth will transform the recognition into a negative one.

You may agree that many patterns in this book should be avoided (or followed, for the positive ones). You may take it a step further and come to the conclusion that it is in your best interest to be *known* for avoiding these patterns, to wear it as a badge of honor. Know that this behavior is a direct contradiction of the pattern described in this chapter. The will to master yourself so you do not fall victim to these patterns cannot be predicated on being recognized for it. Your personal sense of discipline must be a foundation on its own. The stool on which you stand to be seen from afar is a wobbly one, and will tumble easily. The bedrock you create for yourself, however, the one that no one will see, never shatters.

Situational Questions

- How much weight do you put into how you are judged or ranked by someone else? If you are ranked lower than you expect, does it change what you know about yourself? Does it change the direction your choices take you?

- Do you brag about doing things *fast* or in large quantity? Is the quality of the action secondary in your consideration? What is more important to you, doing something first (or many times over), or doing it well?

- Do you go to great lengths to establish a legacy for yourself? Is the narrative with which you are remembered more important than the truth behind your accomplishments? If you were to cease trying to manipulate such perception, what new endeavors could your energy be applied to?

Personal Example

As I write this, I have no idea whether it will be read by anyone. Maybe I'll share it with some family members I'm comfortable with. Maybe it will resonate with someone I've never met before. Who knows? Better question is: who cares? The primary purpose of these words is for me to have a medium to express my ideas and better understand them for myself. A prerequisite for attempting this book was that recognition would not be a measurement of success.

That is not to say I don't dream of this actually having a positive effect on others. I have an ego just like anyone else, and as I write, my mind unwittingly wanders towards a reality where I am recognized for it. The important point is that I make sure these **dark** thoughts that I cannot control don't translate into actions that cause me to fall into the pattern I'm describing here.

❧ Reciprocity ❧

I look for guidance
Amongst my dreams
I sit in silence
My body steams
The mist it rises
An angel forms
While in my crisis
She came adorned
She speaks no words
Her eyes they pierce
Her wings they spread
Her might is fierce
Her fury brings
Me to my knees
She sees the things
I try to keep
I look inside
To find the answer
I know this time
It will outlast her
A feather floats
Across my face
My neck it slopes
From all the weight
What has she gifted?
I look behind
The weight is lifted
These wings are mine

Step outside yourself.

Several patterns have been discussed in this book, and many of them overlap in some way. Undoubtedly, there will be other patterns that you see in your own life, that may or may not be connected to what has been laid out here. Even within these patterns there will be characteristics that others will think of. It is impossible to try to anticipate every situation, and it is worse to try to formulate complex rules to follow, rules that will inevitably need to be revisited as times change. Rigid dogma prevents you from adapting to circumstances as they become known, and forces you to be on the defensive when any new idea is introduced.

Certainly there must be a simple, common thread that binds these patterns together. Something that allows you to eventually derive each aspect of them, no matter where in the thought process you might start. Something that, through your own reflection, without the direction of others, allows you to come to the right decision for yourself. Something flexible enough to withstand the endless variations of situations that we all may face. To explore this, I would offer that each of the patterns in this book can be summarized in a particular way. A way that asks: how would you react to someone else's behavior? Let's see:

- You would probably respect someone who finds joy in discovery, who finds more worth in the journey than the end.

- You would probably respect someone who didn't get caught up in formality, or try to impose formality on you.

- You would probably respect someone who didn't try to fit in, and who didn't try to make you fit in.

- You would probably respect someone who found the intrigue in every experience, and made connections to their own life.

- You would probably respect someone who constantly absorbed their surroundings and strove to understand every detail.

- You would probably respect someone who wasn't afraid to genuinely approach who they were in awe of, or who was awestruck by them.

- You would probably respect someone who kept their composure where others might panic.

- You would probably respect someone who didn't keep things unnecessarily private, but still respected your privacy.

- You would probably respect someone who always remained honest.

- You would probably respect someone who didn't waste any time being inactive.

- You would probably respect someone who valued listening over talking, and gave purpose to each of their words.

- You would probably respect someone who admitted their mistakes and wasn't afraid of failure.

- You would probably respect someone who always sought out challenges and never became dependent on luxury.

- You would probably respect someone who pursued what they truly desired, and didn't ask others to relinquish that right.

- You would probably respect someone who didn't give up on someone else, who worked to look for the diamond in the rough.

- You would probably respect someone who never believed they couldn't accomplish their goals, who tirelessly strove for mastery.

- You would probably respect someone who rejected the idea of perfection.

- You would probably respect someone who didn't overdramatize the small things.

- You would probably respect someone who didn't try to avoid debating their ideas, or validate your conclusions for their own benefit.

- You would probably respect someone who was steadfast with their decisions, but agile enough to absorb new information.

- You would probably respect someone who didn't presume you did something that you didn't actually do.

- You would probably respect someone who didn't resent you for something you were unconsciously doing.

- You would probably respect someone who exercised the power of their choice to change their situation.

- You would probably respect someone who didn't have a sense of superiority, and tried to learn from every interaction.

- You would probably respect someone who never let their dark thoughts turn into dark actions, but also didn't needlessly fight with their mind.

- You would probably respect someone who didn't look for recognition, but still went out of their way to recognize you.

Every pattern, every potential pattern, and how you should act in each situation, can be derived from the simple idea of reciprocity. Imagine your actions being taken by someone else, and think about what your reaction to them would be. To be clear, I am not saying imagine what *their* reaction would be—their opinion in this case is meaningless. Given your own full understanding of your situation, how would you react to someone else doing the same thing? Only you can provide that answer. It certainly may be the case that you disagree with many of the observations in this book. That is perfectly alright, as long as you are reciprocating what you expect of someone else in your shoes.

The standards you set for yourself must not be influenced by the tides of the masses. People around you will be making decisions based on their own situations, their own outlook of the world. You may find reprieve in following the crowd, in allowing your own discipline to be relaxed when others are so openly bending theirs. But, as has been mentioned many times in this book, the only actions you are ever fully in control of are your own. The actions of others are not a justification for what you do and how you do it. The choice will always be yours and yours alone. If you can step outside your body, and play the role of a spectator who has every ounce of context at their disposal, and can judge accurately whether they approve, you will have a compass that *always* steers you in the right direction. It is a compass that will lead you down the path of breaking the perpetual pattern.

Acknowledgments

I am extremely grateful to all my family, friends, and co-workers that took the time to give me feedback on this book. This is my first foray into writing and their encouragement and support when I shared my first draft was amazingly helpful. People went out of their way to help me find mistakes and improve the work. I received a wide range of honest opinions, which helped me realize it was important to keep the different aspects of each chapter intact so there may be something everyone could connect with. It was my hope to approach this as a do-it-yourself project, to forgo the normal editing and publishing process. The feedback and help I received from friends and family was instrumental in allowing that to happen.

I would like to give special thanks to my parents. They've always cultivated an environment for me with no barriers on where I could let my mind explore. Any opportunity that I have been lucky enough to take advantage of is because of the support they've given me. Many of the best lessons in these chapters come from the examples they have set. My father's inexhaustible positivity and energy has taught me to never back down from a challenge. My mother's unbounded love and compassion has taught me to see the beauty in everything.

I also want to mention my mother's father, Pashauri Lal Jauhar, who is an amazing writer and poet. He has always encouraged my cousins and I in anything we've attempted, and doesn't have a negative bone in his body. Whatever poetic blood I might have in me comes straight from him. He has always had the confidence to share his poetry with any audience and doesn't shy away from any topic. I would like to think my mind has grown to work similar to his in observing the things around us, and finding a way to profoundly express the reflections that follow.

Thank you to everyone who helped me see this project to fruition.

www.ingramcontent.com/pod-product-compliance
Lightning Source LLC
Chambersburg PA
CBHW060820050426
42449CB00008B/1748